Gender-Neutral Fashion: Redefining Style and Breaking Barriers

Abdul   Latif   Kadir

DEDICATION

I dedicate this book to Almighty God for life and how far he has brought me. To my loving family,

This book is dedicated to each and every one of you who has stood by my side, offering unwavering love and support throughout my writing journey. Your presence in my life has been a constant source of strength and inspiration.

To my parents, who instilled in me a love for words and storytelling from an early age, thank you for nurturing my creative spirit and always believing in my dreams. Your guidance and encouragement have shaped me into the writer I am today.

To my siblings, whose unwavering belief in me has been a constant source of motivation, thank you for cheering me on, challenging me to grow, and reminding me of the importance of perseverance. Your presence has been a pillar of strength throughout this writing process.
This book is a testament to the love, sacrifices, and encouragement you have poured into my life. Your unwavering presence has fueled my determination, and I am eternally grateful for the unwavering support you have shown me.

With heartfelt appreciation,

Contents

ACKNOWLEDGMENTS

I would like to express my sincere gratitude to the following individuals who have contributed to the realization of this book:

First and foremost, I am deeply indebted to my mentor and guide, Nuzrat Owusu. Your wisdom, expertise, and unwavering belief in my abilities have been instrumental in shaping this work. Your guidance and invaluable feedback have been transformative, and I am forever grateful for the knowledge and insights you have imparted upon me.

I would like to acknowledge the contributions of my colleagues and peers, whose valuable discussions and intellectual exchanges have stimulated my thinking and helped refine my ideas. Your perspectives have broadened my horizons and deepened the significance of the topics explored in this book.

I am indebted to the reviewers and editors who have meticulously reviewed and provided constructive feedback on the manuscript. Your insights and suggestions have immensely contributed to the quality and clarity of this work.

A special word of thanks goes to my family and friends for their unwavering support, patience, and understanding throughout the writing process. Your love and encouragement have been my constant motivation, and I am grateful for your belief in me.

Lastly, I would like to express my gratitude to the readers of this book. Your interest, engagement, and feedback are invaluable. It is my sincere hope that this work resonates with you, sparks new ideas, and fosters meaningful discussions.

Without the contributions and support of these remarkable individuals, this book would not have come to fruition. I am profoundly grateful for their presence in my life and their impact on this work.

Thank you all for being an integral part of this journey.

INTRODUCTION

I am pleased to welcome you to "Gender-Neutral Fashion: Redefining Style and Breaking Barriers." In this eBook, we explore a progressive and revolutionary fashion industry movement that welcomes diversity and questions long-held gender conventions.

A. Definition and Significance of Gender-Neutral Fashion

Gender-neutral fashion, also known as unisex or non-binary fashion, refers to a style that transcends the limitations of the gender binary. It encompasses designs, clothing, and accessories that are not confined to stereotypical masculine or feminine presentations. Instead, gender-neutral fashion embraces a spectrum of expression and empowers individuals to dress in a way that aligns with their personal identity, regardless of societal expectations.

The significance of gender-neutral fashion lies in its ability to redefine style, liberate individuals from societal constraints, and foster a more inclusive and diverse fashion landscape. It challenges the long-held notion that clothing should be strictly categorized based on gender, opening doors for self-expression and creativity beyond prescribed norms.

B. Historical Context and Evolution of Gender Norms in Fashion

To understand the rise of gender-neutral fashion, we delve into its historical context and the evolution of gender norms within the fashion industry. Throughout history, fashion has been used as a tool to reinforce and reflect societal ideals of gender roles. Traditional gendered fashion has perpetuated stereotypes and limited self-expression. However, over the years, fashion has witnessed shifts in attitudes and the breaking down of gender boundaries.

C. Purpose of the Book: Explore the Concept, Challenges, and Opportunities of Gender-Neutral Fashion

The purpose of this book is to delve deep into the concept of gender-neutral fashion, examining its significance, understanding its nuances, and highlighting the challenges and opportunities it presents. We will explore the multifaceted dimensions of gender-neutral fashion, from its defiance of traditional gender norms to its intersectionality with social factors such as race and culture.

Through various chapters, we will discuss the role of fashion in shaping personal and cultural identities and showcase empowering case studies of individuals and communities embracing gender-neutral fashion. We will also delve into the design aspect, challenging stereotypes, and exploring sustainable and ethical practices in gender-neutral fashion design.

Furthermore, we will analyze the fashion industry's response to gender-neutral fashion, from representation and inclusivity efforts to collaborations and partnerships fostering a more inclusive industry. The evolving consumer mindset, market trends, and retail strategies will be explored in relation to gender-neutral fashion consumption. Additionally, we will examine the intersection of fashion and social activism, addressing issues like cultural appropriation and highlighting initiatives that promote inclusivity and diversity.

Finally, we will look toward the future of gender-neutral fashion, discussing technological advancements, education, and awareness efforts that promote understanding and acceptance. Predictions and visions for a more inclusive fashion industry will be shared, inspiring readers to embrace diversity, break gender barriers, and actively support the growth of gender-neutral fashion.

Join us on this enlightening journey as we celebrate the power of gender-neutral fashion to redefine style, break barriers, and pave the way for a more inclusive.

2 CHAPTER UNDERSTANDING GENDER-NEUTRAL FASHION

A. The Role of Fashion in Shaping Personal and Cultural Identities

Fashion holds immense power in shaping personal and cultural identities. Throughout history, clothing has served as a means of self-expression, signaling one's beliefs, values, and affiliations. Gender-neutral fashion plays a significant role in this process by challenging societal norms and offering individuals the opportunity to present themselves authentically, regardless of gender expectations.

Within the realm of gender-neutral fashion, individuals can explore and redefine their identities, finding a sense of liberation and empowerment. The rejection of traditional gender norms allows for a broader spectrum of self-discovery and expression. By transcending the limitations imposed by binary fashion, gender-neutral fashion provides a platform for individuals to truly embrace their uniqueness and showcase their multifaceted identities.

Moreover, gender-neutral fashion has a profound impact on cultural identities. It creates space for cultural expression beyond gender stereotypes, allowing individuals from diverse backgrounds to reclaim their heritage and intertwine it with their personal style. By dismantling the rigid boundaries imposed by traditional gendered fashion, gender-neutral fashion encourages cultural inclusivity and celebrates the richness of diverse traditions.

B. Self-Expression and Empowerment through Gender-Neutral Fashion

Gender-neutral fashion serves as a powerful tool for self-expression, enabling individuals to communicate their innermost thoughts, emotions, and identities. By defying traditional gender norms, individuals can dress in a way that aligns with their true selves, unrestricted by societal expectations. The freedom to choose garments and accessories regardless of their assigned gender allows for a personalized and authentic mode of self-expression.

Furthermore, gender-neutral fashion empowers individuals to reject societal pressures and take control of their own narratives. It enables them to challenge societal norms, break free from stereotypes, and embrace their individuality with confidence. By embracing gender-neutral fashion, individuals can create a personal style that reflects their unique journey, passions, and aspirations, empowering them to navigate the world on their terms.

C. Case Studies: Individuals and Communities Embracing Gender-Neutral Fashion

To understand the impact of gender-neutral fashion on individuals and communities, we explore compelling case studies that highlight diverse experiences and perspectives. These case studies shed light on the transformative power of gender-neutral fashion and showcase how it has revolutionized the lives of those who have embraced it.

We will meet individuals who have found solace, acceptance, and personal growth through gender-neutral fashion. Their stories will provide insight into their journeys of self-discovery, the challenges they faced, and the triumphs they experienced by embracing a gender-neutral wardrobe. We will witness how gender-neutral fashion has allowed them to express their true selves, build confidence, and find a supportive community.

Additionally, we will explore the collective efforts of communities and organizations that advocate for gender-neutral fashion. From fashion collectives and designers challenging the status quo to grassroots movements promoting inclusivity, we will examine the impact of these initiatives on fostering a more accepting and diverse fashion landscape. These case studies will demonstrate the power of solidarity and community-building in driving social change.

By delving into these case studies, we gain a deeper understanding of the personal and collective transformations that occur when individuals and communities embrace gender-neutral fashion. Their stories serve as beacons of inspiration, illustrating the potential for growth, self-acceptance, and empowerment that lies within gender-neutral fashion.

In Chapter 2, we have explored the profound role that fashion plays in shaping personal and cultural identities. We have examined how gender-neutral fashion facilitates self-expression and empowers individuals to break free from societal expectations. Through inspiring case studies, we have witnessed the transformative impact of gender-neutral fashion on individuals and communities. As we move forward, we will delve into the design aspect of gender-neutral fashion, challenging stereotypes, and exploring sustainable and ethical practices in gender-neutral fashion design.

3 CHAPTER FASHION AND IDENTITY

A. The Role of Fashion in Shaping Personal and Cultural Identities

Fashion serves as a powerful tool in shaping personal and cultural identities. It goes beyond mere aesthetics, as the clothes we wear can communicate our values, beliefs, and aspirations. In the realm of gender-neutral fashion, this role becomes even more significant, as it allows individuals to express their authentic selves without conforming to traditional gender expectations.

By embracing gender-neutral fashion, individuals can challenge and redefine societal norms, freeing themselves from the constraints of prescribed gender roles. Fashion becomes a means of self-discovery and self-expression, enabling individuals to showcase their true identities and break free from the limitations imposed by binary fashion.

Moreover, gender-neutral fashion plays a vital role in shaping cultural identities. It allows individuals from diverse backgrounds to honor and express their heritage without conforming to gender stereotypes. By rejecting traditional gender norms in fashion, cultural communities can reclaim their traditions and incorporate them into their personal styles, fostering a more inclusive and diverse cultural landscape.

B. Self-Expression and Empowerment through Gender-Neutral Fashion

Gender-neutral fashion provides a platform for self-expression and empowerment, allowing individuals to authentically present themselves to the world. By defying traditional gender norms, individuals can transcend societal expectations and embrace a style that resonates with their true selves.

Through gender-neutral fashion, individuals can communicate

their values, beliefs, and unique perspectives. It becomes a form of non-verbal communication that empowers them to showcase their individuality and challenge the limitations placed on their identities. By choosing garments and accessories that align with their personal preferences rather than societal norms, individuals can create a wardrobe that reflects their true essence.

In addition, gender-neutral fashion fosters a sense of empowerment by enabling individuals to reclaim agency over their own bodies and identities. By rejecting the notion that clothing should be confined to specific genders, individuals can take control of their self-presentation and reject the pressures of conforming to societal expectations. This empowerment extends beyond fashion choices, influencing various aspects of individuals' lives and relationships.

C. Case Studies: Individuals and Communities Embracing Gender-Neutral Fashion

To further understand the impact of gender-neutral fashion on identity, we explore compelling case studies of individuals and communities who have embraced this transformative movement.

Through these case studies, we encounter individuals who have discovered a sense of liberation and self-acceptance through gender-neutral fashion. Their stories illuminate the ways in which their fashion choices have allowed them to express their true identities, navigate societal challenges, and build confidence. We witness how gender-neutral fashion has provided them with a platform for self-expression, enabling them to create a personal style that aligns with their unique journey.

Furthermore, we explore the experiences of communities and organizations that have embraced gender-neutral fashion as a means of fostering inclusivity and empowering marginalized groups. We delve into the collective efforts that support and celebrate diverse identities, showcasing how gender-neutral fashion has become a catalyst for social change and empowerment.

By examining these case studies, we gain insights into the profound impact of gender-neutral fashion on personal and cultural identities. They serve as inspirations for readers, highlighting the transformative power of fashion in embracing one's true self and celebrating diversity.

In Chapter 3, we have explored the pivotal role of fashion in shaping personal and cultural identities. We have examined how gender-neutral fashion facilitates self-expression and empowerment, providing individuals with a platform to challenge societal norms. Through engaging case studies, we have witnessed the transformative impact of gender-ncutral fashion on individuals and communities. As we progress, we will delve into the design aspect of gender-neutral fashion, challenging stereotypes, and exploring sustainable and ethical practices in gender-neutral fashion design.

4 CHAPTER: DESIGNING GENDER-NEUTRAL FASHION

A. Fashion Design beyond Gender: Blurring Boundaries and Challenging Stereotypes

Designing gender-neutral fashion involves going beyond the constraints of traditional gender categories and challenging societal stereotypes. It requires a mindset that rejects the notion of clothing as inherently gendered and instead embraces inclusivity and fluidity in design.

Fashion designers have the opportunity to create garments that are not confined to binary expectations, allowing individuals to express their true selves. By blurring the boundaries between masculine and feminine aesthetics, designers can challenge preconceived notions of what constitutes "appropriate" clothing for different genders.

Designing gender-neutral fashion also involves breaking free from stereotypes associated with specific gender presentations. It means offering a diverse range of styles that cater to individual preferences and expressions, irrespective of societal expectations. By doing so, designers contribute to a more inclusive and diverse fashion landscape that celebrates the multiplicity of identities.

B. Fabrics, Silhouettes, and Colors That Transcend Traditional Gender Categories

In gender-neutral fashion, the choice of fabrics, silhouettes, and colors plays a crucial role in transcending traditional gender categories. Designers can explore materials that are not inherently associated with a specific gender, allowing for greater versatility and freedom in clothing choices.

Fabrics that are soft, comfortable, and adaptable can be utilized to create garments that suit a variety of body types and expressions. The emphasis should be on promoting individual comfort and self-expression, rather than adhering to rigid gender norms.

Similarly, the choice of silhouettes should be inclusive, accommodating a range of body shapes and sizes. Designers can experiment with cuts that emphasize fluidity, allowing garments to be worn by individuals regardless of their gender identity or expression.

Color palettes in gender-neutral fashion should transcend traditional associations with masculinity or femininity. By embracing a diverse range of hues, designers create opportunities for individuals to select colors that resonate with their personal style and expression, rather than conforming to societal expectations.

C. Sustainable and Ethical Practices in Gender-Neutral Fashion Design

In the pursuit of gender-neutral fashion, it is crucial to prioritize sustainable and ethical practices. Designers have a responsibility to consider the environmental and social impact of their creations.

Sustainable practices in gender-neutral fashion design involve using eco-friendly materials, adopting responsible production processes, and promoting circularity. Designers can explore organic, recycled, or upcycled fabrics, reducing the industry's reliance on environmentally harmful materials. Additionally, prioritizing ethical manufacturing practices ensures fair wages and safe working conditions for garment workers.

Designers should also consider the longevity of their designs, creating pieces that are timeless rather than driven by fast fashion trends. By encouraging longevity and versatility, designers contribute to reducing waste and promoting a more sustainable fashion industry.

Furthermore, gender-neutral fashion should embrace inclusivity in its sizing and fit options. Designers can work towards creating clothing that caters to a diverse range of body types and sizes, ensuring that everyone has access to well-fitting and stylish garments.

By incorporating sustainable and ethical practices into gender-neutral fashion design, designers pave the way for a more responsible and compassionate industry that respects both people and the planet.

In Chapter 4, we have explored the world of designing gender-neutral fashion. We have discussed the importance of blurring boundaries and challenging stereotypes, allowing fashion to go beyond gendered expectations. By focusing on fabrics, silhouettes, and colors that transcend traditional gender categories, designers create opportunities for individual expression. Lastly, we have emphasized the significance of sustainable and ethical practices in gender-neutral fashion design, promoting a responsible and inclusive industry. As we continue, we will delve into the representation and inclusivity efforts in the fashion industry, highlighting brands and initiatives that lead the way in embracing gender-neutral fashion

5 CHAPTER FASHION INDUSTRY AND GENDER-NEUTRAL FASHION

A. Representation in the Fashion Industry: Breaking Barriers and Promoting Inclusivity

Representation plays a pivotal role in promoting inclusivity and breaking down barriers within the fashion industry. Gender-neutral fashion challenges traditional norms and seeks to provide a space where individuals of all gender identities can see themselves represented.

By increasing representation, the fashion industry can reflect the diversity of its consumers, fostering a sense of belonging and acceptance. This involves featuring models of different genders, body types, ethnicities, and backgrounds in campaigns, runway shows, and editorials. By showcasing the beauty and uniqueness of individuals embracing gender-neutral fashion, the industry can inspire others and challenge societal norms.

B. Fashion Brands Leading the Way: Examples of Gender-Neutral Fashion Pioneers

In recent years, numerous fashion brands have emerged as pioneers in the realm of gender-neutral fashion. These brands challenge traditional fashion conventions and prioritize inclusivity, making significant contributions to the industry's transformation.

Through innovative designs and marketing strategies, these brands demonstrate that gender-neutral fashion is not merely a trend but a movement towards a more inclusive future. They showcase the versatility of gender-neutral garments and emphasize the importance of individual self-expression. By incorporating diverse models and collaborating with underrepresented communities, these brands exemplify the power of fashion as a catalyst for social change.

C. Collaborations and Partnerships for a More Inclusive Industry

To further advance the cause of gender-neutral fashion, collaborations and partnerships play a vital role. When brands, designers, organizations, and communities join forces, they create a more inclusive industry and amplify their impact.

Collaborations between established brands and emerging designers in the gender-neutral fashion space allow for the exchange of ideas and expertise, fostering innovation and pushing boundaries. Partnerships with organizations advocating for gender inclusivity enable the fashion industry to align itself with larger social movements and promote positive change.

Additionally, collaborations between the fashion industry and LGBTQ+ organizations, cultural communities, and grassroots initiatives ensure that the voices and experiences of marginalized groups are represented and uplifted. By working together, these collaborations contribute to a more inclusive and equitable industry, where gender-neutral fashion is celebrated and embraced.

Through increased representation, the emergence of gender-neutral fashion pioneers, and collaborative efforts, the fashion industry can become a catalyst for change. By embracing and promoting gender-neutral fashion, the industry breaks barriers and fosters inclusivity, creating a space where individuals of all gender identities can express themselves authentically.

In Chapter 5, we have explored the relationship between the fashion industry and gender-neutral fashion. We have discussed the importance of representation in breaking barriers and promoting inclusivity within the industry. Additionally, we have highlighted fashion brands that lead the way in embracing gender-neutral fashion and inspiring change. Finally, we have emphasized the significance of collaborations and partnerships in creating a more inclusive industry. As we move forward, we will delve into the consumer mindset, market trends, and retail strategies surrounding gender-neutral fashion.

6 CHAPTER FASHION CONSUMPTION AND GENDER-NEUTRAL FASHION

A. The Evolving Consumer Mindset: Demand for Gender-Neutral Options

Fashion consumption is undergoing a significant shift as consumers embrace the concept of gender-neutral fashion. The evolving consumer mindset reflects a growing demand for clothing options that transcend traditional gender categories.

Individuals are seeking garments that allow them to express their authentic selves without conforming to prescribed gender norms.

They are increasingly aware of the limitations imposed by binary fashion and are seeking inclusive alternatives that resonate with their personal identities.

The demand for gender-neutral options extends beyond the LGBTQ+ community, as people from various backgrounds and identities are embracing this movement. Consumers recognize that gender-neutral fashion promotes diversity, inclusivity, and self-expression, leading to a more liberated and accepting society.

B. Market Trends and the Commercial Viability of Gender-Neutral Fashion

Market trends indicate that gender-neutral fashion has gained significant commercial viability. Fashion brands and retailers are recognizing the potential and economic opportunities that come with embracing gender-neutral designs.

As consumers increasingly seek gender-neutral options, fashion brands are expanding their offerings to cater to this growing market segment. From established brands to emerging designers, the fashion industry is incorporating gender-neutral elements into their collections, blurring the boundaries between traditional gender categories.

Moreover, market research shows that gender-neutral fashion appeals to a broad range of consumers, regardless of their gender identity. This inclusivity translates into increased sales and brand loyalty, as customers feel seen, respected, and represented through gender-neutral fashion offerings.

C. Retail Strategies and Marketing Campaigns for Gender-Neutral Fashion

Retailers are adopting various strategies and marketing campaigns to promote gender-neutral fashion and cater to the evolving consumer preferences.

Firstly, brands are reevaluating their store layouts and merchandising techniques to create a more inclusive and gender-neutral shopping experience. They are moving away from gender-specific sections and instead organizing their collections by style, fit, or occasion, allowing customers to explore options based on their personal preferences rather than societal expectations.

Additionally, marketing campaigns play a crucial role in promoting gender-neutral fashion. Brands are challenging gender norms through their advertising, featuring diverse models and showcasing garments in a way that appeals to a wide range of identities. These campaigns highlight the inclusivity and self-expression that gender-neutral fashion enables, resonating with consumers who seek authentic representation.

Moreover, online platforms and social media have become powerful tools for connecting with consumers and promoting gender-neutral fashion. Influencers, bloggers, and online communities play a vital role in amplifying the message of inclusivity and spreading awareness about gender-neutral fashion options.

By adopting inclusive retail strategies and engaging marketing campaigns, brands and retailers create an environment that celebrates diversity and empowers individuals to embrace gender-neutral fashion.

In Chapter 6, we have explored the dynamic relationship between fashion consumption and gender-neutral fashion. We have discussed the evolving consumer mindset and the growing demand for gender-neutral options. Market trends indicate the commercial viability of gender-neutral fashion, and retailers are adapting their strategies and marketing campaigns to cater to this demand. As we continue, we will delve into the role of fashion as a platform for social activism and explore initiatives and movements in the gender-neutral fashion space.

7 CHAPTER THE FUTURE OF GENDER-NEUTRAL FASHION

A. Technological Advancements and the Digital Revolution in Gender-Neutral Fashion

The future of gender-neutral fashion is intertwined with technological advancements and the digital revolution. Technology has the potential to revolutionize the way we design, produce, and consume fashion, opening up new possibilities for gender-neutral expressions.

Virtual reality (VR) and augmented reality (AR) technologies can enable individuals to try on and customize gender-neutral garments virtually, breaking the constraints of traditional fitting rooms. This immersive experience allows for greater personalization and exploration of diverse styles and designs.

Advancements in 3D printing and digital fabrication offer opportunities for on-demand production, reducing waste and enabling customized gender-neutral fashion. These technologies allow designers and consumers to create unique garments that reflect individual preferences, identities, and body types.

Furthermore, social media and online platforms play a significant role in the future of gender-neutral fashion. Digital spaces provide a platform for diverse voices and allow for the democratization of fashion, where emerging designers and communities can showcase their creations and challenge traditional norms.

B. Education and Awareness: Promoting Understanding and Acceptance of Gender-Neutral Fashion

Education and awareness are essential for promoting understanding and acceptance of gender-neutral fashion. As society continues to evolve, it is crucial to foster an inclusive environment where individuals are educated about gender diversity and the significance of gender-neutral fashion.

Educational institutions, fashion schools, and industry professionals can play a role in incorporating gender-neutral fashion into curricula, workshops, and training programs. By integrating discussions around gender identity, expression, and inclusivity, we can equip future designers and industry leaders with the knowledge and tools to embrace and celebrate gender-neutral fashion.

Public awareness campaigns, media representation, and community engagement also contribute to promoting acceptance of gender-neutral fashion. By highlighting the experiences and stories of individuals who embrace gender-neutral fashion, we can challenge stereotypes, combat discrimination, and foster empathy and understanding.

C. Predictions and Visions for a More Inclusive Fashion Industry

The future holds exciting possibilities for a more inclusive fashion industry, where gender-neutral fashion becomes a norm rather than an exception. Here are some predictions and visions for this inclusive future:

1. Gender-Inclusive Runways: Fashion weeks and runway shows will increasingly feature gender-inclusive collections, showcasing designs that cater to diverse identities and expressions. Runways will become platforms for celebrating inclusivity and pushing the boundaries of traditional gender norms.

2. Collaborative Design: Designers will collaborate with communities and individuals from diverse backgrounds to co-create gender-neutral collections that reflect a multitude of identities and cultural influences. This collaborative approach will promote cultural exchange, representation, and respect within the fashion industry.

3. Mainstream Integration: Gender-neutral fashion will become more integrated into mainstream retail spaces, breaking away from the confines of niche markets. Traditional retailers will expand their offerings to include gender-neutral sections, acknowledging the growing demand and ensuring accessibility for all consumers.

4. Sustainable Practices: The future of gender-neutral fashion will prioritize sustainability, with designers and brands adopting eco-friendly materials, circular production models, and ethical practices. The industry will embrace responsible fashion as an integral part of gender-neutral fashion, furthering the progress towards a more sustainable future.

By embracing technological advancements, fostering education and awareness, and envisioning a more inclusive fashion industry, we can shape a future where gender-neutral fashion is celebrated and accessible to all. In the final chapter, we will recap the key points discussed throughout the book, reflect on the transformative power of gender-neutral fashion, and issue a call to action for embracing diversity, breaking gender barriers, and promoting inclusive fashion.

8 CHAPTER CONCLUSION
A. Recap of Key Points Discussed in the Book

Throughout this book, we have embarked on a journey to explore the world of gender-neutral fashion and its transformative power. We have examined various aspects, delving into the definition and significance of gender-neutral fashion, its historical context, and the challenges and opportunities it presents.

We explored the concept of gender-neutral fashion, discussing its ability to defy traditional gender norms, embrace a spectrum of gender identities and expressions, and intersect with other social factors such as race and culture. We recognized the role of fashion in shaping personal and cultural identities and the empowering nature of self-expression through gender-neutral fashion.

Furthermore, we examined the design principles of gender-neutral fashion, focusing on how it blurs boundaries, challenges stereotypes, and embraces sustainable and ethical practices. We explored the role of the fashion industry in promoting inclusivity, breaking barriers, and featuring gender-neutral fashion pioneers. Additionally, we discussed the evolving consumer mindset, market trends, and retail strategies surrounding gender-neutral fashion.

B. Final Thoughts on the Transformative Power of Gender-Neutral Fashion

Gender-neutral fashion has the transformative power to redefine style and break barriers. It challenges the limitations imposed by traditional binary fashion, allowing individuals to express their authentic selves beyond societal expectations. By embracing gender-neutral fashion, we promote diversity, inclusivity, and acceptance.

This movement goes beyond mere clothing choices; it symbolizes a larger societal shift towards a more equitable and inclusive world. Gender-neutral fashion empowers individuals to embrace their unique identities, fosters a sense of belonging, and celebrates the beauty of diversity.

Through gender-neutral fashion, we can reshape the fashion industry as a platform for social activism, cultural appreciation, and positive change. It enables us to challenge norms, break down gender barriers, and build a more inclusive society where everyone can freely express themselves.

C. Call to Action: Embracing Diversity, Breaking Gender Barriers, and Promoting Inclusive Fashion

As we conclude this book, I urge you to take action and be part of the movement towards a more inclusive fashion industry and society at large. Embrace diversity, challenge gender norms, and promote inclusive fashion in the following ways:

1. Educate yourself and others: Continuously educate yourself about gender diversity, inclusivity, and the experiences of marginalized communities. Share this knowledge with others to foster understanding and empathy.

2. Support Gender-Neutral Fashion Brands and Designers: Seek out and support fashion brands and designers that prioritize gender-neutral fashion and promote inclusivity. By voting with your wallet, you can drive change and encourage the industry to embrace diversity.

3. Advocate for Representation: Demand increased representation of diverse genders, body types, and identities in the fashion industry. Support campaigns and initiatives that promote inclusive representation and challenge harmful stereotypes.

4. Foster Inclusivity in Your Communities: Create spaces and communities that celebrate and embrace gender diversity. Encourage dialogue, acceptance, and respect for all identities and expressions.

5. Embrace Self-Expression: Embrace your own self-expression through fashion, regardless of societal expectations or norms. Wear what makes you feel confident and authentic, and encourage others to do the same.

By taking these actions, we can collectively shape a more inclusive future, where gender-neutral fashion becomes the norm rather than the exception. Let us continue to break down barriers, challenge norms, and celebrate the beauty of diversity through the transformative power of gender-neutral fashion.

In closing, I invite you to carry forward the knowledge and insights gained from this book and actively contribute to redefining style, breaking barriers, and promoting an inclusive fashion industry. Together, we can create a world where fashion truly knows no bounds and where everyone is free to express themselves authentically.